MW00511089

CRICUT MAKER FOR BEGINNERS

The Step-by-Step Guide to Master Your Cutting Machine, Easy to Follow Even if You Have Never Used it Before.
A Handbook with Simple Tips, Illustrations &
Screenshots

Milly Cooper

Table of Contents

Introduction 7

Chapter 1: How to choose the right machine for your needs . 10

Criteria for Choosing a Cricut Machine 11

Quick Overview of the Main Models 14

Cricut Maker 16

Cricut Joy 18

Cricut Compare Models 20

Difference in Models 22

Chapter 2: Cricut Maker 24

Machine Setup and How to Prepare the Material 24

Cartridge 27

Loading Your Paper 28

How to Remove Your Cuts from Cutting Mat 30

How to design With Cricut Maker 33

How to Clean The Cricut Maker 36

Cricut Design Space software For Cricut Maker 38

Making Your First Project Idea 42

How to Upload Images with a Cricut Maker 46

Cut Vinyl with A Cricut Maker.. 51

How to Make Stickers.. 53

Procedure for Making Cupcake Stickers 53

Procedures for Making Sticky Labels.. 55

Working With Images/Edit Panel.. 57

Cricut Scrapbooking... 63

Solving the most common problem when using Cricut Maker . 64

Chapter 3: Cricut Joy.. 68

Machine Setup and How to Prepare the Material...................... 68

Cartridge... 74

Loading Your Paper 76

How to Remove Your Cuts from Cutting Mat 79

How to design With Cricut Joy... 80

How to Clean The Cricut Joy 81

There are many ways to clean your cutting mat. 83

Cricut Design Space software For Cricut Joy 87

Making Your First Project Idea 91

How to Upload Images with A Cricut Joy................................. 94

Cut Vinyl with a Cricut Joy 96

How to Make Stickers.. 96

Working With Images/Edit Panel 101

Cricut Scrapbooking...103

Solving the most common problem when using Cricut Joy......106

Chapter 4: FAQs about the Cricut Maker & Joy...................111

Why does Design Space say my Cricut machine is already in use when it's not? 111

Why doesn't my cut match the preview in Design Space? 111

What do I do if I need to install USB drivers for my Cricut machine? 112

Why does my Cricut Maker say the blade is not detected?........113

Why is my Cricut machine making a grinding noise? 113

Why is my mat going into the machine crooked? 114

Why isn't the Smart Set Dial changing the material in Design Space?..114

What do I do if my Cricut Maker stopped partway through a cut? 115

Why is my fabric getting caught under the rollers?...................116

Why would my Cricut Maker continuously turn off during cuts? 116

Chapter 5: Tips that might Assist You To Begin 117

Make sure that you have a deep cut blade.................................117

Know your glue... 118

Think about a Coach.. 119

Exhibit Your True Talent with a Business Card for Artists 119

Give the Quality of Your Work a chance to radiate through... 120

Consider Other Ways You Can Display Your Skills to the World
.... 120

Remember to tell individuals how to connect!........................... 121

Be Adaptable 121

Conclusion **123**

Introduction

Okay, you've bought a Cricut machine, and you are excited. You have thought so much on what you are going to do with it. Now you have it. You really don't know the process. Well, that is why I am here. We would talk extensively about Cricut project ideas.

Whatever you have in mind, maybe you want to become this craftsperson, or you just want to do it for fun in a school or office we have several ideas for you here

You can buy these machines from an online store or at a craft store. And the price would definitely depend upon the model you choose. Furthermore, the prince can range anywhere from $100-$350 (and above), so it is better you narrow down your needs and go for it. Whatever makes your work more comfortable and efficient can be regarded as a significant investment. The Cricut is one of them; it is rewarding and fun to use. Anyone can benefit from it. Because of its efficiency, we have Cricut in places we never envisioned that they would be in previous years.

We have Cricut in offices and workshops. Does that sound strange to you? It shouldn't be because Cricut is never meant to be a home-only tool. It is time-saving and makes your work so professional, and the beautiful thing about it is that there are no limits to it, you can do whatever you can. If you're reading this book, then you have a Cricut machine in your possession, and maybe you don't really know how to use it. Well, I am here to help you with that.

First, we have the Cricut maker which is a machine used with design space. This Cricut maker has a cloud-based online software. And this particular series or design cannot function alone you would need to use the design space on a desktop or a laptop computing, and of course, internet connection is needed.

Another special provision provided with the Cricut maker is that you can make use of the offline feature in the design space app whenever you're using the design app on an IOS device, i.e., an iPad/iPhone or MacBook. This means you can make designs and all without an internet connection. This is just one device, and that is not all because each device has its own peculiarities added to the general feature that we all know. We also have the Cricut Explore Air.

This invention of Robert Workman with the collaboration of fellow investors like Jonathan Johnson, Matt Strong, and Phil Beffrey is also pronounced as cricket. This product has been able to gather so many revenues in sales within a short period of time because of its effectiveness and handiness.

This machine has been in work for years, and it totally blows everyone's mind and any other cutting machine out there. They keep bringing more and more to the table, and they keep adding something new every now and then. The Cricut has been able to dominate that market because of its reliability, performance, durability and its firmware also. This force of paper crafting revolution can also work without being connected or hooked to a computer. There are some designs that are portable and convenient to carry. Are you thinking of creating an endless assortment of shapes, letters, and phrases? Don't think too far, just get a Cricut.

Chapter 1: How to choose the right machine for your needs

On the whole, your choice of model depends on the type of use you will be giving it. This is the main criteria to take into consideration. If you are a casual hobbyist, then you might want to get the basic model. This will allow you to avoid spending more than you'd like while getting all of the benefits from the Cricut Machine. If you are planning on using it for business purposes, then it might be best to consider getting the top of the line model.

With that in mind, let's take a look at the criteria that we can take into consideration when purchasing a Cricut Machine. So, your answer to the following questions will help you make a decision on which model is the most suitable for you.

Criteria for Choosing a Cricut Machine

Here are five questions that you ought to ask yourself when looking to purchase your first Cricut Machine. Be honest as the answers to these questions will reveal the right model for you. That way, you can get the most out of your Cricut Machine without breaking the bank.

What am I going to use it for?

If you are a casual hobbyist and crafter, that is, you don't plan to use the machine heavily, the Explore Air model would suit you just fine. This model offers all of the capabilities that the other models offer though it isn't quite as robust as the others. This is perfect if you don't plan to use it heavily, such as cutting a large number of items in one go. It's perfect if you are looking to cut one or two items at a time.

On the other hand, if you are looking to make heavy use of the machine, such as in the case of business use, then the Cricut Maker may be the best option for you. While it's the priciest, it's also the fastest and most robust of the lot. Given the fact that it's the most

11

powerful model, you'll be able to cut anything and produce a large number of items in a short time.

How much am I willing to spend on a Cricut Machine?

On the other hand, if you are looking for a more budget-friendly solution, then the Explore Air makes the most sense. As we have stated earlier, if you are looking to avoid spending a great deal of money, then you can even pick up a used one. Since the Cricut Machine is pretty solid, you won't have to worry about it being in bad shape. Of course, it depends on how it was treated by its previous owner. But on the whole, they are usually in pretty good shape, especially if it doesn't have a lot of mileage on it.

If you are looking to purchase it for business purposes, then you might want to consider the Cricut Maker. It offers all of the features you need and will handle any workload you throw its way. While any of the other models will do the trick, the Maker is by far the fastest machine. In the world of business, time is certainly an important consideration. So, it only makes sense to get the fastest machine available to you.

Should I upgrade my Cricut Machine?

Assuming you have already taken the plunge with your first Cricut Machine, you might consider upgrading your current model. This is especially true if the breadth and scope of your projects have outgrown your current machine.

A note of caution though: if you are looking for serious power, then getting the Maker is the best way to go. However, it isn't recommended to get it used, at least not if you're looking to upgrade for serious use. The reason for this is that the Maker is a powerful machine, but it may be put through the wringer. So, getting a brand-new makes sense if you're considering putting some serious mileage on it. Alternatively, the Joy can be a great upgrade, particularly if you something smaller to work with.

What add-ons can I get with the Cricut Machine?

When you get a Cricut Machine, you get access to any number of add-ons and tools which can be used to make any number of creations. These add-ons consist of pens, cartridges, and other tools that can be used to make effects beyond the standard cutting function. Cricut has gone a long way toward making a vast array of

13

tools available. That's something that can't be said about other similar kinds of machines on the market.

It is worth paying close attention to the chapter in which we will discuss the types of tools available to you. That way, you can see for yourself just how many options you have available. In the end, the Cricut Machine offers the best balance in terms of capability and function. You can create plenty of designs while working with several techniques. When you put it all together, the overall capabilities of the Cricut Machine place it at the top of its category.

Quick Overview of the Main Models

The Cricut Machine is one of the most sophisticated tools that can be used in the world of arts and crafts. It allows you to make a myriad of creations by combining its specially designed software and then translate it into a physical form of art.

In essence, the Cricut Machine is a cutting machine. It can cut any number of materials based on predetermined patterns that you develop in the specially designed software. In these creations, you can take a material, and have the Cricut Machine cut out the patterns you want it to.

Now, it should be noted that this device is meant to cut only. It doesn't do any printing. So, that's an important thing to keep in mind. For instance, you can cut out an elaborate design on a piece of leather and then color it to your liking. If you are making a birthday card, you can cut out the design you like and then color it using your technique of choice (pastels, crayons, paints, watercolors, and so on).

That being said, the Cricut Machine is a great tool for any type of project. You can go as elaborate as you like. The important thing is to make sure you have the right idea in mind. Based on that, you can make anything work for you.

Cricut Maker

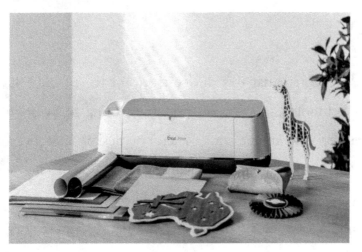

The Cricut Maker is the first and only device from Cricut that can be used with a Rotary blade to cut fabrics directly. It is also equipped with a scoring wheel that can exert varying pressure to allow scoring of thicker papers. It provides the most diverse variety of tools to cut, score, write, and even decorate; so you can truly bring your dream projects to life. Moreover, the company is looking to add even more tools that can be used with Cricut Maker and quickly switched to support your creative growth continually.

With the versatile housing slot, you can just press the "quick release" button on the device to mount any desired tip and kick start your craft project.

Features:

- Fast and precision cut creating a rotary blade.

- Use the knife blade to cut thin as well as thick materials.

- Use 12 x 12 inches cutting mats with fine point pen.

- It offers a number of digital sewing patterns.

- Use your own designs.

- It comes with a device docking slot.

- Equipped with Bluetooth wireless technology.

- A USB port allows charging your mobile devices while in use.

Cricut Joy

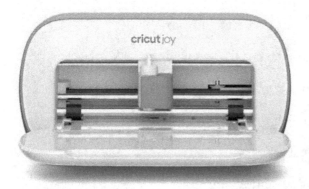

It's the most up to date machine Cricut discharged. It's very small and it can cut, draw a wide assortment of materials. the Cricut Joy can cut and remove vinyl and iron-on without a tangle!

You may have the option to buy them on amazon or utilized. In any case, they are not good with Cricut Design Space and the product they used previously – Cricut Craft Room – has been closed down totally. Composing with your Cricut is so natural and fun. It's an extraordinary method to give an undertaking proficient introduction with an individual and custom made feel.

On the off chance that you sew a great deal it might simply be justified, despite all the trouble to have that rotating shaper. Also, how cool is it to have wood patterns? Words cut in wood are overly popular at this moment. Furthermore, who realizes what number of more apparatuses Cricut will come out with that will just work in the   Maker.

Cricut Compare Models

Cricut is exploring one, Cricut Explore Aire, Cricut, and Cricut Explore Air 2 Maker.

With these options, you might be wondering what the differences between them are and what to buy.

I will explore these models and then briefly explain the Cricut machines should be used depending on the depth on the ship.

Cutting force

The machine comes with a carbide blade premium German first category, which can be cut through thick materials and light equally clearly and cleanly form. Even if exploring one is recommended for beginners, it is very professional. The blade is also very durable.

As for the width of cutting, explore one can cut sizes ranging from 23

½ "high and ¼ to ½" 11 wide.

Although the explore one looks excellent, there are some activities that can be done in the design space Cricut if you are using this model.

20

Cricut Design Space is very user-friendly when used to explore one. It accepts .jpg, .png, and .bmp.

In addition, the Cricut Explore One cannot work wirelessly. To add comfort to it and does not care about the cost, then you can buy a Bluetooth adapter and use it to transfer images or files wirelessly.

Explore Cricut Air

While this is quite similar to the Explore One model, which also comes with some additional features, the main difference between them is the presence of the built-in Bluetooth adapter. If you enjoy seeing no cables and wires around your workplace, especially with the risk of tripping over them, then this model solves that problem.

Capacity

Explore air is also exploring different ones as it has a double carriage. This means that you can draw, write, or record while mowing because it has two clamps to hold both tools. This saves you money because you do not have to buy an adapter tool.

Materials

Explore air is quite liberating when it comes to materials. It features a dial that can allow you to choose the material you are about to cut. This way, you do not have to guess the depth of the blade and spoil the material.

The machine will know how deeply felt the need to cut and what kind you have to be paper or vinyl. This is especially great for beginners' feature that they are not well versed in the depths of the sheet.

Difference in Models

In general, there is no difference between the three models of Cricut Machine. They are all capable of cutting out the same types of patterns and materials. As such, may casual hobbyists would instead go for the Joy (especially when looking affordability and portability) or the Explore Air (especially when looking for an excellent entry-level product). However, it's the Maker that shines when it comes to using all of the tools available. By using the Maker, you have the opportunity to unlock the power of the Cricut Machine. It can cut through thicker and stricter material while allowing you the versatility of the various tools we outlined in the previous chapter.

If you are seriously considering the Cricut Machine for heavy-duty crafting or business purposes, then the Maker makes the most sense. After all, it will provide you with the best all-around features and value. Sure, the price is the highest, but in the end, the large array of projects you will be able to carry out will may the machine worth the investment.

Additionally, you will find that the size of the materials will vary between the Joy and Explore Air/Maker. Given the fact that the Joy is much smaller, you are only able to cut materials roughly half the size of the other two machines. This is something which you need to keep in mind if you are considering the Joy. Otherwise, any of the three models will provide you with excellent results.

Chapter 2: Cricut Maker

Machine Setup and How to Prepare the Material

First, you'll want to set up the Cricut Joy. To begin, create a space for it. A craft room is the best place for this, but if you're at a loss of where to put it, I suggest setting it up in a dining room if possible. Make sure you have an outlet nearby or a reliable extension cord.

Next, read the instructions. Often, you can jump right in and begin using the equipment, but with Cricut machines, it can be very tedious.

Make sure that you do have ample free space around the machine itself, because you will be loading mats in and out and you'll need that little bit of wiggle room.

The next thing to set up is, of course, the computer where the designs will be created. Make sure that whatever medium you're using has an internet connection, since you'll need to download the Cricut Design Space app. If it's a machine earlier than the Explore

24

Air 2, it will need to be plugged in directly, but if it's a wireless machine like the Air 2, you can simply link this up to your computer, and from there, design what you need to design.

Imputing Cartridges and Keypad

The first cut that you'll be doing does involve keypad input and cartridges, and these are usually done with the "Enjoy Card" project you get right away. So, once everything is set up, choose this project, and from there, you can use the tools and the accessories within the project.

You will need to set the smart dial before you get started making your projects. This is on the right side of the Explore Air 2, and it's basically the way you choose your materials. Turn the dial to whatever type of material you want, since this does help with ensuring you've got the right blade settings. There are even half settings for those in-between projects.

For example, let's say you have some light cardstock. You can choose that setting, or the adjacent half setting. Once this is selected in Design Space, your machine will automatically adjust to the correct location.

You can also choose the fast mode, which is in the "set, load, go" area on the screen, and you can then check the position of the box under the indicator for dial position. Then, press this and make your cut. However, fast mode is incredibly loud, so be careful.

Once it's confirmed, you can go to images, and click the cartridges option to find the ones that you want to make. You can filter the cartridges to figure out what you need, and you can check out your images tab for any other cartridges that are purchased or uploaded.

You can get digital cartridges, which means you buy them online and choose the images directly from your available options. They aren't physical, so there is no linking required.

Cartridge

Cartridges are expensive, they truly are, but they are so easy and fun to use as well. Cartridges contain a huge amount of images and fonts. They are all themed so they can be purchased according to what you need them for. Some cartridges only contain letters, and these have really cool fonts that can be used to write on cards or cut with your machine. Each one of them also has a fair amount of options that will allow you to customize the design as much as you want.

You will need to link the cartridge of the new machines to the Design Space; hence, an internet connection is necessary if you wish to work with them within the application itself. The older machines do not have such a requirement, but the upgraded ones do. So, either way, you will need an internet connection for linking the cartridges or setting up with Design Space.

Loading Your Paper

To load paper into a Cricut machine, you'll want to make sure that the form is at least three inches by three inches. Otherwise, it won't cut very well. You should use regular paper for this.

Now, to make this work, you need to put the paper onto the cutting mat. You should have one of those, so take it right now and remove the attached film. Put a corner of the form to the area where you are directed to align the paper corners. From there, push the form directly onto the cutting mat for proper adherence. Once you do that, you just load it into the machine, following the arrows. You'll want to keep the paper firmly on the mat.

Press the "load paper" key that you see as you do this. If it doesn't take for some reason, press the unload paper key, and try this again until it shows up.

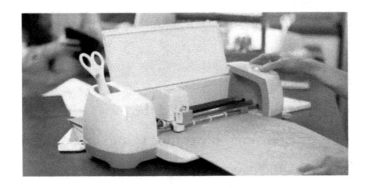

Now, before you do any cutting for your design, you should always have a test cut in place. Some people don't do this, but it's incredibly helpful when learning how to use a Cricut. Otherwise, you won't get the pressure correct in some cases, so get in the habit of doing it for your pieces.

For effective cutting, it is recommended that the paper to be cut should not be lesser than 3" × 3". Cardstock is also recommended in order to achieve the best result. In case you are using the machine for the first time, you can become familiar with the device by practicing with cheaper materials.

In order to cut a paper on the machine, the form should be placed on the cutting mat. It is better to first try it with a form of 6" × 12" if you are not used to the machine. First, remove the protective film of the cutting mat.

You will then ensure that a corner of the paper is aligned. Proceed by pressing the writing unto the cutting mat to make it fit in well. Once this is done, the paper is ready to be cut. In case you want to choose other paper sizes, check the Advanced Operations.

How to Remove Your Cuts from Cutting Mat

The machine will automatically load the mat and the paper after pressing the load paper key. In the rare occurrence that this does not happen, don't hesitate to push the Unload Paper key.

Once you press the Unload Paper key, you will go through the procedure again. It should work unless there is an issue with the machine. A likely problem is the unavailability of up to 1 ft. (30.5 cm) of clear space.

This clear space is needed in the front and back of the Cricut machine for paper movement.

Removing your cut from the mat is easy, but complicated. Personally, I ran into the issue of it being more involved with vinyl projects since they love to just stick around there. But we'll explain how you can create significant cuts and remove them, as well.

The first thing to remember is to make sure that you're using the right mat. The light grip ones are good for very soft material, with the pink one being one of the strongest, and only to be used with the Cricut Maker. Once the design is cut, you'll probably be eager about removing the project directly from the mat, but one of the problems with this is that often, the project will be ruined if you're not careful. Instead of pulling the project from the mat itself, bend the mat within your hand, and push it away from the project, since this will loosen it from the carpet. Bend this both horizontally and vertically, so that the adhesive releases the project.

Use this spatula to lightly pull on the vinyl, until you can grab it from the corner and lift it up. Otherwise, you risk curling it or tearing the mat, which is what we don't want.

You will notice that Cricut mats are incredibly sticky, and if you don't have a Cricut spatula on hand or don't want to spend the money, metal spatulas will work, too. You can put the paper on a flat surface and then lightly remove it. But always be careful when removing these items.

How to design With Cricut Maker

When you see the finished product from a Cricut machine, you will definitely be blown away. The neatness and appealing look of a typical project done with the Cricut machine will take your breath away. However, only a few people understand the process involved in the creation of such unique designs.

Curious to know how the Cricut machine is able to cut out materials effectively? You are reading the right book. There are three significant steps involved when using the Cricut machine:

Have a Design

If you have a PC, you can access the Cricut Design Space to access the library of designs. If you have a Mac, you can access the same platform to select a vast variety of formats. In case you don't have any of these two but possesses an iPhone or iPad, you can use the Design Space for iOS.

If what you have is an android, you are covered as well. This is because you can take advantage of the Design Space for Android.

These are online platforms where you can select any design that best suits your taste.

You can also customize a ready-made design to suit your need. For example, you can resize it or modify the shape. You can also add a text or image as you wish till you have the design just as you want it.

Prepare the Machine

Having selected the design, you intend cutting out with the machine, you are ready for the next step. The device needs to be prepared by turning it on. Once you switch on the device, you actually don't need to do anything.

You don't have to press any button unless you are using the machine for the first time. In that case, the device will give you instructions on what to do. It is that simple.

That is why both beginners and experts can make use of the Cricut machine without issues. Your computer or phone will have to be paired with the device via Bluetooth for the first time. However, this will not be needed subsequently because the machine will remember the pairing.

Hence, once the machine is switched on, the pairing between the phone and the machine becomes automatic. The implication of this is that once the machine is switched on, the machine is ready. The next step is to send the design to the machine.

Send the Design to the Machine

This is the last stage of the process of cutting with the Cricut machine. Once the machine is powered on, at the top right corner of the screen, you will see the Make It button. This button is a big green button on the Cricut Design Space.

The first thing the software does is to preview the various mats you have. A mat represents a sheet of material; hence, having two different colors in your project implies two rugs. There are times that your project can be a combination of a fabric and a paper.

The machine will request that you pick the particular material you want to use for the first mat. Simply choose whether it is paper, vinyl, fabric, leather, or any other material. Once you do this, the machine will automatically adjust pressure, speed, and the brush blade as necessary.

Hence, just ensure you do your part of instructing the machine to do your bidding as desired. You can trust the Cricut machine from that point to do all that is needed for a perfect project. After the machine has adjusted itself to cut, you will put the material into the Cricut cutting mat.

It is obvious that you don't have to be a genius before you are qualified to use the machine. The instructions are simplified such that anyone who can understand basic English language can use it. Therefore, if you have been thinking that you might not be able to operate this machine, you are wrong.

How to Clean The Cricut Maker

With an extended period of use, it is likely that your machine would have collected dirt and grime. So, here are some tips on how you can clean your machine and keep it looking and working as new.

Prior to cleaning the machine, make sure that it has been powered off and disconnected from the power source.

Use a microfiber cloth or a piece of soft clean cloth sprayed with a glass cleaning solution to clean the machine.

In the case of static electricity build-up on the machine due to dust or paper particles, use the same cloth to wipe off the residues and get rid of the static from the machine.

For grease build up on the bar that allows the carriage travels, use a soft cloth or tissue or cotton swab and gently remove the oil from the machine.

Do not use nail polish remover or any other acetone-containing solution to clean the machine, as it may permanently damage the plastic shell of the machine.

To keep the machine running smoothly, you may want to grease it following the instructions below:

Power off your machine and carefully push the "Cut Smart" carriage to the left of the machine.

Use a tissue to wipe the carriage bar (located in front of the belt).

Now, carefully move the bar to the right and clean again with the tissue.

Carefully move the bar to the center and use a cotton swab to lubricate both sides of the carriage by applying a light coating of grease around the bar to form a 1/4-inch ring on each side of the carriage.

In order to evenly distribute the grease on the carriage, slowly move the carriage from one end to another a couple of times and wipe off any excessive oil.

Note – It is recommended to use grease packet supplied by Cricut only, and no other grease from a third party should be used.

Cricut Design Space software For Cricut Maker

For craft enthusiasts and people that love the Cricut die cutting system, it is no longer news that digital die cutting units are incredibly restrictive.

They mostly allow users to cut a small number of fonts and they are not cheap at all.

Thankfully, there are a few programs out there that have managed to open Cricut to enable them to cut designs, True Type fonts created by users and many more.

Below is a list of the best third-party software to use with Cricut.

Make the Cut

This is an excellent third- party Cricut Design software that comes with simple but highly effective design features e.g. it packs quick lattice tools, and it can convert raster images into vectors for cutting. The program has been around for some time. Some of the most outstanding features of the tool include;

It comes with advanced editing tools, and it is quite easy to use (even for a newbie) because the user interface is effortless to learn.

The software works with many file formats and it also uses TrueType fonts

The software comes with Pixel trace tool that allows users to take and convert raster graphics into vector paths for cutting.

Make The Cut is a user-friendly and flexible Cricut related software that adds more utility to the digital die cutting machine that is usually limited in terms of usage and application.

Sure Cuts A Lot

The Sure Cuts A Lot software gives users complete control of their designs without the restrictions of cartridges featured in Cricut DesignStudio.

Users must install a firmware update to their Cricut die cutting machine; however, they can do this for free by downloading the trial version of DesignStudio. It is a straightforward task to perform.

Some of the features of the Sure Cuts A lot software include;

It allows users to use the OpenType and TrueType fonts.

It is the one and only Cricut Design tool available that comes with freestyle drawing tools.

It allows users to create unique designs with basic drawing and editing tools.

The program works with Silhouette, Craft ROBO, and Wishblade die cutting machines.

It is specifically designed to open up all of Cricut's cutting features and abilities.

It allows users to edit the individual nodes the make up the path.

It comes with an auto trace feature that converts raster graphics into vector images

Cricut DesignStudio

Cricut DesignStudio, a product of ProvoCraft is a program that allows users to connect Cricut to a personal computer so that they can do much more with Cricut fonts and shapes.

For those that don't know, Provo Craft is the same company that manufactures Cricut die cutting machines. With the aid of various tools, this Cricut software allows users to adjust fonts and shapes.

Some of the best features of the software include;

Users have the option of previewing and creating designs with different images from the Cricut library.

Users will have to purchase a cartridge to cut.

The software comes with a high level of customization to the Cricut library, and the extra features are beneficial

People that use this software are still limited to the same shapes and fonts from the cartridges they own, but bearing in mind the tools that are packed in the program, that is not an issue.

The program remains a perfect option to use alongside your Cricut, and you'll be able to get the best out of its features. To know more about the software, go to their official website.

Making Your First Project Idea

Now that you have everything set to go, it's time to start with your first project. If this is the first time that you are using a Cricut Machine, then do follow the guidelines we will be presenting in this chapter as they will help you avoid some of the most common mistakes.

On the whole, using a Cricut Machine and the Design Space software is pretty straightforward. This means that you don't need any specialized knowledge to make fair use of this software. Of course, if you have used design software in the past, then that experience will certainly come in handy. Nevertheless, you don't need to have any previous experience to make your creations come to life.

So, here are five useful tips that you can put into practice when starting with your very first projects.

Do your homework

When starting out, it's always a good idea to go over sample project ideas before you actually start cutting. In this book, you will find great project ideas which you can put into practice right away. Do, it's a great idea to go over these ideas before you begin designing your creations. In addition, the internet is filled with great design ideas. So, you can poach some of these ideas and use them for your benefit. On the whole, there are really talented and creative designers out there who have come up with sample projects to help new users get the hang of the Cricut Machine.

As you gain more practice and proficiency with the Cricut Machine, it's a good idea to keep perusing project ideas. It could be that you find images which you can later customize to your own liking. This will make it easier for you to get the hang of the types of projects you can come up with. Over time, you will be able to make your ideas from scratch!

Start small

When you don't have much experience with the Cricut Machine and Design Space, it's a good idea to start with small projects. Such projects don't take up a lot of time and are easy to put together. As you gain more experience and proficiency, you can tackle bigger and bigger projects. But when starting out, it's always a good idea to tackle smaller projects. That way, you won't become overwhelmed by the complexity of a larger project.

Also, it's essential to consider that if things don't go quite as planned, you won't feel frustrated by this. So, you will be able to manage your skills and expectations in such a way that you won't get discouraged early on.

Practice makes perfect

Like anything in life, becoming a pro with the Cricut Machine and Design Space take time and practice. Now, this doesn't mean that you need weeks and weeks of training and study. What it does mean is that the more projects you take on, the easier it will become to use the Cricut Machine and Design Space. So, it definitely helps to take on more and more projects.

Of course, we all have pretty tight schedules nowadays. So, it's not precisely simple to sit down at your computer and work for hours on end on projects. Yet, if you can dedicate a couple of hours a week to your projects, you will find that it will really help you get the most out of the Cricut Machine. In this manner, you will quickly build up your proficiency. Before you know it, you will be coming up with genuinely creative and innovative ideas.

Easy does it

One of the first reactions that newbies to the Cricut Machine get is to be gung-ho about using their brand-new machine. However, enthusiasm tends to wear off. This is why it's a good idea to take on one project at a time. You see, when you get ahead of yourself and take on multiple projects at once, things can get a bit muddled. While there is nothing wrong with being aggressive and trying to make the most out of your new machine, taking on multiple projects early on can be a bit confusing and potentially overwhelming. This might even lead you to feel discouraged. So, the perfect antidote to this point is to take on one project at a time. The sense of satisfaction that you get from completing your very first projects is indescribable.

Draw out your idea on paper first

Design Space is a fantastic tool. It is the perfect companion that enables you to translate the ideas in your head to practical applications. As such, you can put its instruments to fair use without much complication and with relative ease.

However, one of the most significant setbacks that first-time users run into is not having a clear picture in their minds about what they would like to do. This can lead you to feel dissatisfied with your creations. Also, it can make finalizing a design a bit challenging.

This is why we recommend that you sketch out your idea on a piece of paper first. This will help you to organize your thoughts before hitting Design Space. While the finished product may differ significantly, it certainly helps to have a good idea of what you plan to do. This technique is similar to what writers do with a storyboard. They outline the story before writing. That way, they know where they will begin and where they will end. If they change their mind along the way, that's fine. The main point is to avoid having your ideas go down paths that won't lead anywhere practical.

How to Upload Images with a Cricut Maker

There are many images to choose from in the library, but it also encourages the use of your images. Images are categorized into two types. The first type is Image, and the second is the Pattern.

Images:

Images also have two types, Basic and the other one is Vector.

Necessary images like JPG, GIF, PNG, are uploaded as one layer.
Uploading the image will require a few steps that the software will
guide through. There are two ways to use the picture.

First, by print and cut features, print the image and then calibrate
the Cricut to cut around it.

Second, is to cut only the outer edges of the image directly on the
machine.

Vector files come in SVG Dxf files, which are not uploaded as a
single layer but multiple layers. Other imported images from

47

different software can also be uploaded. You can search the uploaded image by searching its name/tag. Also, all uploaded images can be seen by applying the filter uploaded.

Pattern:

Uploaded patterns can be seen in the Layers Attributes Panel under the Pattern option. Files that can be uploaded are .jpg .png .gif .bmp. When uploading, choose appropriate tags and name for easy searching. You can also access this by clicking uploaded in Patterns filter.

How to upload an image from Photoshop?

Cricut Design Space does not allow you to make changes to the images that you want to use. If changes are to be made to the design, then another software like Adobe Photoshop should be used first. Adobe Photoshop does not save vector files, so if the picture has multiple layers, it will be compressed into one. Images best work in jpg. Files, but others can also be used.

Firstly make the required changes in the image using Photoshop. Then save the file in jpg. Format and name it.

How to select an image?

It is effortless to select an image onto the Canvas. There are four methods for this task:

First, select an image from inside the Canvas. When an image is selected, it will be shown in the Layers Panel in the highlighted form, and a bounding box will appear around the image.

Or, select an image from the Layers Panel. This will also like the print on your Canvas

Another option is to select an image from drawing a box. Then draw a box around the idea that it is entirely inside it. The package will turn blue, and the image will be selected.

If there is one image, select the 'Select All' option. If there is more than one image, then all of them will be chosen.

Working with uploaded photos

Select the option for upload images under the upload page

If it is a photo, then select the option 'Complex Image' under the upload screen. Then click 'Continue.'

For the photo to retain its details, it should be used in print and cut. It is done by default, and it is saved as print and cut image. Now click save.

Back on your upload screen, click on the photo and then click insert. The image is now ready to use.

This photo can be manipulated using different tools such as slip tool, or flatten tool. The slip tool can be used to cut the picture or cut images out of the photo. The flatten tool can insert different pictures on the photo.

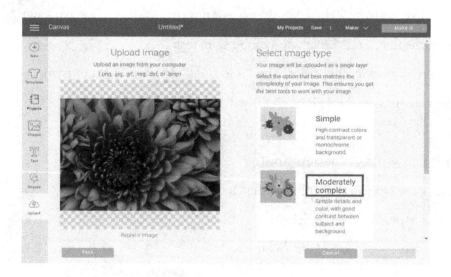

Patterns

Select the option for upload pattern under the upload screen.

Browse the photo using its name and selected.

Name and add appropriate tags to your photo to make searching easy.

A shape can be used to cut the image to make a pattern. First, insert a form in the Canvas. Open the 'Layers Attributes Panel' under the 'Image Layers' option. Now select 'Line Types' and then 'Patterns.' Different patterns will open along with the photo. Select the desired photo and fill the shape.

Use different editing tools to your likings, like rotate, scale, pan, and mirror.

Cut Vinyl with A Cricut Maker

First, place the Vinyl liner side down onto the Standard grip mat. Then put it inside the machine after selecting the design. Push the go button to start.

For a smooth placement of the vinyl, you should use vinyl transfer tape. Transfer tape is a kind of pre-mask that transfer vinyl graphics to a substrate after being cut and weeded.

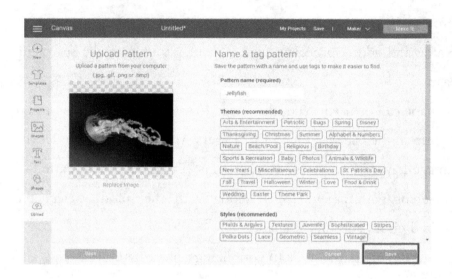

After cutting is done, remove the negatives of the image by a weeder or a tweezer, only leaving the wanted design on the mat. Now remove the Transfer Tape liner. Carefully with the sticky side down, place it on the mat with the system. Gently press to remove any air bubbles.

Whatever surface you want the design on, it should be clean and dry. Carefully place the vinyl on the body and gently press it down. Remove the tap by peeling it off at a 45-degree angle. If it is difficult, burnish it by using a scrapper.

How to Make Stickers

There are a lot of designs and decors one can use the Cricut machine to create. Some of the stickers one can use the machine to create and cut are as follows:

- Cupcake stickers

- Sticky labels

- Planner stickers

- Safari animal sticker

- Vinyl sticker for car windows amid any other types of sticker your heart so desires

Now let us explore individual designs that can be effected with the machine.

Procedure for Making Cupcake Stickers

The supplies needed for this brand of stickers are:

- the Cricut machine,

- printable sticker paper,

- an inkjet printer.

53

The following are the steps to follow in creating cupcake stickers:

- Log in to the Cricut design spaces.

- Start a new project and click on the Images icon on the left side of the screen.

- Select the cupcake image(s) you want.

- Highlight the whole image and use the Flatten button to solidify the image as one whole piece.

- Resize the image to the appropriate size you need. You realize this by clicking on the image then dragging the right side of the box to the size you desire.

- Click Save at the top left to save your project. Save it to be a Print and Cut image, after which you click the Make It button at the right hand of the screen.

- Examine the end result and click Continue if it's what you expected. This will lead you to print the design onto the paper.

- Adjust the dial on the Cricut machine to the required settings.

- Place the sticker paper on the cutting mat.

- Load the cutting mat into the machine, and push it against the rollers.

- Press the Load/Unload button and then the Go button to cut the stickers.

- Sit back and relax while you watch the Cricut machine cut your designed stickers for you.

Procedures for Making Sticky Labels

Supplies needed are as follows:

- Cricut machine
- Printable sticker paper
- Inkjet printer

Take the next few steps to bring this sticker to life:

- Log in to the Cricut design space.
- Start a new project.
- Click on the Text icon and input your text.
- Select the font of your desire from the available font package.
- Highlight the texts and change the color by using the available colors on the color tray.

- Click on the Print option to change the file to a print file from a cut file.

- Click on the Ungroup icon to adjust the spacing of the text. After adjusting the spaces, highlight all and use the Group icon to make them one whole piece again.

- Click on the Shape icon and insert a shape.

- If it's a rectangle you need, insert a square, unlock the shape, and drag it to a rectangle.

- Change the shape's color using the color tray.

- Highlight the text and use the Align drop-down box.

- Make use of the Move to Front icon to move the text to front.

- Highlight the design and click on Group.

- Duplicate the label as much as you want.

- Highlight the whole design and use the Flatten icon to keep it together during printing.

- Highlight the design and right-click then select Attach.

- Click on the Go button and print the design on the printable sticker paper.

- Adjust the dial on the Cricut machine to the required settings.

- Place the sticker paper on the cutting mat.

- Load the cutting mat into the machine, and push it against the rollers.

- Press the Load/Unload button and then the Go button to cut the stickers.

Your sticky label is ready for use.

Working With Images/Edit Panel

The blank Edit Bar is shown in the picture below. All the functions that can be seen on the Edit Bar are explained right after, so we can get you started on creating your first craft project on Design Space.

Undo/Redo – You can use the "Undo" button to revert to your previous state and use the "Redo" button to perform the step that was undone.

Linetype – All the way, the machine can interact with the design base material on the mat, namely, Cut, Draw, Score, Engrave, Deboss, Perf, and Wavy are called as "Linetype."

Linetype Swatch – If you would like to choose additional layer attributes for your design, you can select the "Linetype swatch." The alternatives available will be updated on the basis of the "Linetype" you selected. When the "Cut" option is chosen, you will notice a solid line next to the "Linetype" icon, an outline if the "Draw" is determined, and when the "Score" is chosen, a "/" will be visible. Here are some details on the features that will be available for your selected "Linetype."

Cut Attributes

Material colors – You can select the desired color on the "Material colors palette" to instantly match the colors of your project. A checkmark will be displayed in the "color swatch" for the design layer that you are working on.

Primary colors – You will also be able to select a color from the "basic color palette."

Advanced – You can move the slider to choose a color from the "custom color picker," or if you know precisely the "hex" numbers for your desired color, simply plug those numbers in, and you will get that color for your design.

Draw Attributes – If you have selected the "Draw" Linetype, you will be given the option to "Choose a Cricut pen type" from the drop-down. The colors available for your selected "pen type" will be displayed in the list accordingly.

Print - You can select this option for accessing "Print Then Cut" color and pattern choices.

Fill Swatch – If you would like to choose from other Fill attributes for a layer, click on the

Original Artwork – If you are not excited about the fill of the design and want to restore to the original image, you can do this by selecting "Original artwork."

Color - You can choose your desired color from the current material colors, a primary colors palette, the custom color picker, or by entering a hex color code.

Pattern - You could also fill an image or text layer with a design. If you filter the pattern selection by color, it will be easier to find the right way, which you can further modify using the "Edit Pattern" tools.

Size – If you need to alter the height or width of an object, then you can simply type in the exact dimensions in the given boxes or click on the "stepper" to increase or decreases the size while looking at the changes on your design. Remember to first lock the image aspect ratio by clicking on the "Lock" icon to ensure that, as you modify one dimension, the whole image will be changed in the same proportion.

Rotate – You will be able to modify the angle of the selected item using the stepper, or you can type in the exact degree by which you want to alter the image.

More – If your screen resolution doesn't allow the complete Edit Bar to be visible, then you would see a "More" drop-down containing the features that do not appear on your screen.

Position – You can use this option to change the status of your selected item using the stepper, or you can type in the exact distance by which you want to move the image from the top-left corner of the Canvas.

Editing Fonts

If you decided to add text to your design or select a "text object" on the Canvas or select a "text layer" in the Layers Panel, the "Text Edit Bar" will be displayed directly below the image "Edit Bar" on your screen. All the functions that can be seen on the "Text Edit Bar" are shown in the picture and explained below.

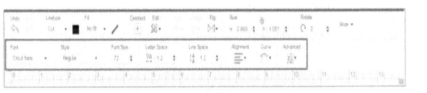

Font – This will provide you a list of Cricut fonts along with all the fonts available on your computer.

Font Drop-Down – You will be able to view all the fonts available to you or may choose to view just the Cricut fonts, or only fonts installed on your system, or all the fonts at the same time, using the "Font Drop-Down." Font filters may also be searched and applied. Just browse the font list and choose your desired font to be applied to the selected text.

Font Filter – You can use this feature for filtering the fonts by category and alter the fonts that are displayed in the "Font Type" menu.

All Fonts – To view all available fonts that can be used for your project.

System Fonts – To view only the fonts installed on your system.

Cricut Fonts – To view just the fonts from the Cricut library.

Single Layer Fonts – To view fonts containing only a single layer.

Writing Style Fonts - To view fonts that are designed particularly to be written by hand. These fonts are characterized by letters with a single stroke that makes them appear like handwritten letters.

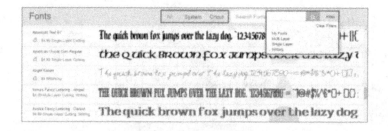

Style – This feature will allow you to select the type of your font, such as regular, bold, italic, and bold italic. You may also see the option of "writing" when the appropriate font has been selected.

Remember, the style of Cricut fonts may differ from your system fonts.

Font Size – You can adjust the size of the fonts by typing in the desired point size or using the stepper to change the font size by 1 point gradually.

Cricut Scrapbooking

Scrapbooking can verge on a fixation for us. We're continually attempting to make that ideal page design or locate that perfect little touch that will make our scrapbooks that significantly improved. You can utilize the Cricut machine to make kick the bucket cuts of scrapbook page formats and afterward rapidly offer them to other fans such as yourself. On the off chance that it is your obsession, at that point it will be no issue thinking of some amazing plans!

Solving the most common problem when using Cricut Maker

Fixing Cricut Design Space Issues

When you put everything into consideration, it is safe to say that the Design Space software is excellent.

No system is perfect, and there's always room for improvements, but on the whole, the software works excellently for several projects. However, there are a couple of related issues that are predominant with the software, including; freezing, slow loading, crashing and not opening at all. When you're faced with these issues, there are several things you can do to fix them, including;

Slow Internet Connection

You must understand that a slow internet connection is one of the leading causes of Design Space problems without saying much. Poor internet connection translates into problems for the software because it requires consistent download and upload speeds to function optimally.

Several websites only require good download speeds e.g. YouTube, thus users on these sites can do away with slow upload speeds. However, unlike those sites, Cricut Design Space requires good upload and download speeds to function optimally because users are always sending and receiving information as they progress with their designs.

Note: If you're using a modem, you're likely to have a more stable connection if you move closer to it.

Run a speed test

You can use a service like Ookla to run an internet speed test.

For Design Space to run optimally, Cricut specifies the following;

- Broadband connection

- Minimum 1 – 2 Mbps Upload

- Minimum 2 – 3 Mbps Download

After running the speed test, if the results are not good, and you are convinced that the connection is affecting to your Design space issues, you should wait until the connection improves or you call your service providers. There is also the option of switching to a new internet service provider with a proper internet connection.

Background Programs

If you're running too many background programs while using Design Space, it might also be a problem.

Some multi-tasking crafters are fond of engaging in different activities while designing on Design Space. For example, some simultaneously chat on Facebook, while downloading movies, watching videos on YouTube, and designing on Design Space. These activities will affect your app and make it malfunction badly, thus it is important to shut down other projects and focus solely on Design Space.

While it is important to close other apps and shut down other activities, there are other things should also do;

- Run a malware check
- If you're using windows, you should upgrade you drivers
- Clear your history and cache
- Defragment your hard drive
- Check your anti-virus software and update if needed

If you execute these tests, it might speed up the system, or even solve all related problems.

Your Browser

Your Design Space software might be having issues due to your system browser.

For you to access Design Space, Cricut recommends using the latest version of the browser you use. Be it Edge, Chrome, Firefox or Mozilla; just make sure that it is up to date. If it refuses to work on a particular browser, open it in another browser to see if it works. Although the reasons are unknown, sometimes its works and even works perfectly.

Contact Cricut

If you've tried all possible options and nothing works, you may have to call Cricut customer care to look into the issues you're faced with.

Chapter 3: Cricut Joy

Machine Setup and How to Prepare the Material

One way or another, you found yourself in possession of a Cricut joy machine and you have been worried about setting it up correctly? Well, there are lots of people like you on this table. Setting up your machine could look somehow complicated or tedious. However, this section is majorly written to guide you through it; the unboxing process and the setting up. So, relax and bring that Cricut machine out wherever you've stashed it. It takes approximately 1 hour to finish setting up a Cricut machine. With this guide, you should be done in less than an hour. Let's get right on it, shall we?

Opening the box

To make sure that we are together all the way through, we will go through even the most trivial step; opening the box.

You should be having a number of boxes right now in front of you if you went for the whole Cricut bundle. And there should be a big box among those boxes which contains the Cricut joy machine itself. If you open that big box, the first thing you should find is a Welcome packet, most of the tools will be in that packet. You should find a welcome book, rotary blade and cover, a USB cable, a fine-point pen, a packet that contains your first die-cutting project. The USB cable is sometimes the last thing you'll see in this packet, it's hidden under every other stuff. Underneath this welcome packet is your Cricut joy machine.

Unwrapping your cricut joy machine and supplies

We are getting to the exciting part. Let's unwrap your machine and find out what's inside.

When trying to unwrap your machine, you'll find it covered in a protective wrapper that looks filmy and also with a cellophane layer. Try to carefully unwrap the top foam layer so you can see the machine. After that, remove the remaining part of the Styrofoam that protects the inner machine housing.

When you unbox the whole casing, you should expect to find the following tools;

- Cricut Machine
- USB and Power Cables

- Rotatory blade with housing.

- Fine point blade with housing

- Fine point pen.

- Light-Grip and Fabric-Grip Mats (12 x 12)

Setting up your cricut joy machine

Once they are all connected, open your computer browser to continue the setup. Visit the **Cricut Sign-in Page** and click on the "Sign in" icon. You will have to either sign in with your account details or create a new account for yourself if you don't already have one. This is necessary so as to be able to access the Cricut

Design Space.

Sign In   Create a Cricut ID

Cricut ID*   . Faster Checkout

your email address   . Save multiple shipping addresses

Password*   . View and track orders and more

Remember Me   Forgot Password?   Create Cricut ID

Sign In

Create a Cricut ID

Your Cricut ID is your golden ticket to all things Cricut

First Name   Email / Cricut ID

Last Name   Retype Email / Cricut ID

Country   Password
  Please select   ∨

☐ I accept the Cricut Terms of use
☑ Send me free inspiration & exclusive offers

Already have a Cricut ID?

If you do not have an active account yet, don't bother to fill any information on the sign-in fields. Click on the "Create Cricut ID" in the green box and then fill out every field with the required information and click on "Submit."

Now, it's time to link your machine to your account. It takes some people a lot of time to finish this part successfully. To make it easier, follow the procedures below.

After signing in, go to the upper left corner of the page and click on the drop-down menu icon (with three lines) beside "Home."

When the drop-down menu appears, select the "New Machine Setup."

On the next screen that pops up, click on your Cricut machine model.

Let's Get Started

Select the product you want to set up, register, or update

Cricut Maker®   Cricut Explore® family

Cricut EasyPress™ 2

Important: Micro USB required

Another webpage will appear with instructions on how to connect your machine. Follow the instruction accordingly.

When you follow the instructions, it automatically detects your machine and prompts you to download and install the software.

The site is user-friendly, so you'll be directed on how to go about the installation. And if you already have an account, you may still need to download it again. Cricut updates their design space often, there could be some new tools in the latest version that you don't have access to. It only takes about five minutes to get the installation done.

Cartridge

Designs are produced using parts put away on cartridges. Every cartridge accompanies a console overlay and guidance booklet. The plastic console overlay demonstrates key determinations for that cartridge as it were. Anyway, as of late Provo Craft has discharged an "All-inclusive Overlay" perfect with all cartridges discharged after August 1, 2013. The motivation behind the all-inclusive overlay is to simplify the way toward slicing by just learning one console overlay instead of learning the overlay for every individual cartridge. Designs can be removed on a PC with the Cricut Design Studio programming, on a USB associated Gypsy machine, or can be legitimately inputted on the Cricut machine utilizing the console overlay. There are two kinds of cartridges shape and textual style. Every cartridge has an assortment of imaginative highlights that can consider several different cuts from only one cartridge.

More than 275 cartridges are accessible (independently from the machine), containing textual styles and shapes, with new ones included monthly. While a few cartridges are conventional in substance, Cricut has to permit Disney, Pixar, Nickelodeon, Sesame

Street, DC Comics and Hello Kitty. The Cricut line has a scope of costs. The cartridges are compatible, even though not all alternatives on a cartridge might be accessible with the little machines. All cartridges work just with Cricut programming. They must be enrolled to a solitary client for use and can't be sold or given away. A cartridge obtained for a suspended machine will probably wind up futile at the point the machine is ended. Cricut maintains whatever authority is needed to suspend support for certain product renditions whenever, which can make a few cartridges quickly out of date.

The Cricut joy Craft Room programming empowers clients to join pictures from different cartridges, consolidate pictures, and stretch/turn pictures; it doesn't take into account the formation of discretionary designs. It additionally empowers the client to see the pictures showed on-screen before starting the cutting procedure so that the final product can be seen in advance.

Loading Your Paper

To load paper into a Cricut machine, you'll want to make sure that the paper is at least three inches by three inches. Otherwise, it won't cut very well. You should use regular paper for this.

Now, to make this work, you need to put the paper onto the cutting mat. You should have one of those, so take it right now and remove the attached film. Put a corner of the paper to the area where you are directed to align the paper corners. From there, push the paper directly onto the cutting mat for proper adherence. Once you do that, you just load it into the machine, following the arrows. You'll want to keep the paper firmly on the mat.

Press the "load paper" key that you see as you do this. If it doesn't take for some reason, press the unload paper key, and try this again until it shows up.

Before you do any cutting for your design, you should always have a test cut in place. Some people don't do this, but it's incredibly helpful when learning how to use a Cricut. Otherwise, you won't get the pressure correct in some cases, so get in the habit of doing it for your pieces.

Selecting Shapes, Letters, and Phrases

When you're creating your Design Space design, you usually begin by using letters, shapes, numbers, or different fonts. These are the basics, and they're incredibly easy.

To make text, you just press the text tool on the left-hand side and type out your text. For example, write the word hello, or joy, or whatever you want to use.

You can choose different Cricut or system fonts, too. Cricut ones will be in green, and if you have Cricut Access, this is a great way to begin using this. You can sort these, too, so you don't end up accidentally paying for a font.

The Cricut ones are supposed to be made for Cricut, so you know they'll look good. Design Space also lets you put them closer together so they can be cut with a singular cut. You can change this by going to line spacing and adjusting as needed.

Adding shapes is pretty easy, as well. In Design Space, choose the shapes option. Once you click it, the window will then pop out, and you'll have a wonderful array of different shapes that you can use with just one click. Choose your shape, and from there, put it in the space. Drag the corners in order to make this bigger or smaller.

There is also the score line, which creates a folding line for you to use. Personally, if you're thinking of trying to make a card at first, I suggest using this.

Once you've chosen the design, it's time for you to start cutting.

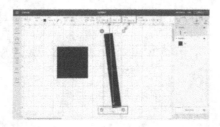

How to Remove Your Cuts from Cutting Mat

For placing your material to cut it on the mat, it's essential to know the placement. First, the mat's cover should be removed and placed elsewhere. The Cricut maker comes with a blue Light Grip mat, which is used for cutting paper mainly. The match will be slightly sticky for the suitable placement of the material. When loading, the material should be placed in the top left corner of the mat. Be sure to press down gently so that the material could be evened out. Place the top of the mat in the guides of the machine. Gently press on the rollers and press the load/to unload the button on top of the Cricut. Once loaded up, the software will tell you the next step. After the project has been finished, the material needs to be unloaded. Press on the load/unload button and take out the mat from the machine. The right way to remove the material from the mat is to be placed on a level surface, and the mat should be peeled off. A scrapper or a tweezer can peel off the remaining scraps.

How to design With Cricut Joy

When you break it down to its most basic operation, the Cricut joy does two things. It cuts, and it draws. However, these two functions have over a million uses and can be used on hundreds of materials, making it a truly versatile crafting powerhouse. Breaking it down to these two features seems almost like an injustice to the adaptability and versatility that this machine truly has.

There are more than 50 crafts you can do using your Cricut joy machine. Here, I will discuss in simple terms these amazing items: Cut fabrics: the rotary blade was designed to cut seamlessly through any fabric including silk, denim, chiffon, and heavy canvass. Coupled with the mat, hundreds of fabrics can be cut without any backing. This is amazing!

Vinyl Decals and stickers: Is cutting vinyl decals and stickers your hobby, then you need Cricut Maker machine as your companion. Get the design inputted in the Design Space Software and instruct the machine to cut. As easy as that. The delivery will be wonderful. So what are you waiting for? Get to work!

Greeting Cards: The power and precision of the Cricut Maker makes cutting of paper and makes greeting cards craft less tedious and saves ample time. Your Christmas cards, birthday cards, success cards and other greeting cards will be delivered with accurate, unique and amazing style.

How to Clean The Cricut Joy

If you want your Cricut machine to last for a long time, you must keep a routine basis. This means appropriately cleaning and maintaining cutting mats and blades.

Cricut machine maintenance

When the Cricut machine is used, eventually, paper particles will inevitably lead to reverse charging, dust, and debris. Also, the fat in the device will begin to stick to the track carriage.

If you want your machine to last long, then you should be cleaned regularly, or otherwise, be damaged prematurely. Here are some cleaning tips to help clean out the engine.

Before cleaning the device, disconnect it from the electrical outlet. This will prevent electrocution or any other accidents that may damage the device or damage.

Apply a small layer of fat on both sides of the carriage smart cut around the bar so that they form a ring is a quarter inch on both sides.

To make fat even become the car, push the smart carriage cut on both sides slowly and repeatedly.

Clean any grease that stained the bar while I was oiling the machine.

You can buy a pack of pasta Cricut. This works better than using a third-party package paste for the machine.

It will not get damaged. This is especially true if the Cricut machine makes a squeaking sound after using another product grease.

This process is almost the same as lubricating the machine maker Cricut too.

Maintaining the Cricut cutting mat

You also have to clean and maintain your Cricut cutting mat because cutting is carried out.

If the cutting is not clean, it can stain the machine. Also, if your cutting mat has left grip, you can spoil your designs and creations.

When your carpet is no longer sticky because of debris and dirt, cleaning and making it sticky again bring back life.

I will mention the solutions that are not ideal for rose-cut mats, just for green, blue, and purple.

There are many ways to clean your cutting mat.

The use of wet wipes for babies:

Make use of baby unscented bleach-free wipes without alcohol to clean your carpet. Must use wipes lighter babies can be found so that no lotions, corn starch, solvent or oil is added to the cutting base. If not, you could affect the adhesion and adhesive carpet. Also, after cleaning, let it dry completely before using it.

Using a sticky lint roller

You can also use a roll of tape if not find a sticky lint roller. Run the roll through the mat to get rid of hair, fibers, dust particles, and paper particles.

Using hot soapy water

You can also clean the carpet with soap and warm water. You must use the flattest possible soap also to not mess with the mat. Use a clean

Cloth, sponge, soft brush, or Magic Eraser. Also, rinse thoroughly and do not use until completely dry.

The use of an adhesive remover

For heavy-duty cleaning, you must use a reliable adhesive remover to clean appropriately. A to use an adhesive remover, read the instructions properly before you start.

Then spray a small amount on the mat and spread with a scraper or anything that can act as a scraper record.

How to make your sticky mat Cut Again

After washing or cleaning, the cutting mat must again make them sticky.

The most advisable way to do their sticky mat is again by adding glue to it. Obtain a solid stick glue-like Zig Pen 2-Way and apply it on the inside of the rug. Then, cerebrovascular accident glues around the mat and make sure there is no residue of glue on the edges of the carpet.

After about 30 minutes, the glue will become clear. If the cutting mat turns out to be too sticky after applying the glue, you can be used a piece of fabric to reduce the adhesive pressing the material into parts of the mat that are very sticky.

You can also use sticky adhesives or spray adhesives that are ideal for cutting mats.

General maintenance

When the carpet is not in use, it is covered with a transparent cover film so that the dust and hair are not accumulated on the surface of the rug.

Carefully manage their mats. If you want to make sure that the adhesive is not damaged, do not touch the sticky surface with your hands.

Always make sure that your carpet to dry completely before using or concealment. Do not use heat when the mat to dry but can be placed in front of a fan. Also, make sure that is drying hang both sides will dry up.

Maintaining the Cricut cutting blade

You can use your Cricut beautiful tip sheet over a year if maintained properly! The same goes for other types of cutting blades. When securing the Cricut cutting blade, you have to keep it sharp all the time, so they do not wear out.

Keep your sharp blade essential because it can damage your materials and waste caused if it is not. Also, if you do not keep your knives, you will have to replace them frequently.

Keeping your blade sharp cut

Extending a portion of an aluminum foil in a cutting mat. Without removing the blade from the casing, cut a simple design on the foil. This sharpening the edge and remove paper particles or stuck on the sheet vinyl. This can be used for any type of cutting blade.

For heavy-duty cleaning, should be squeezed a sheet of foil on a ball. It is necessary to remove the blade housing of the machine to use this method. Then press the

Plunger, making the sheet and paste into the aluminum foil ball repeatedly. You can do this 50 times. This will make it sharper and also remove particles vinyl or paper sheet.

How to save your blade

The best way to store the cutting blade is left in the compartment Cricut. It can be placed in the drop-down door that is in front of the machine. This compartment is intended for storing the sheet.

The blade's case can be placed in the plastic points raised in the back of the machine. There are magnets on the front of the computer where you can paste loose sheets.

When you put your sheets on the Cricut machine, never loses its blades.

Cricut Design Space software For Cricut Joy

Moving on to Creating Your Project Template

On the home page, select "New Project", followed by a page with a blank canvas that looks like the grid on your Cricut mats. The words "empty canvas" is a nightmare in itself to any artist, so please just bear with me since we will fill that bad boy up in a second. But first, let's go through the menu options.

New, Templates, Projects, Images, Text, Shapes, and Upload. These are the things that you will see on your left-hand side when you have the canvas open on the screen.

New

New means that you will start a new project and clicking the tab will redirect you to a blank canvas. Be sure to save all changes on your current project before you go to the new canvas. Otherwise, you will lose all of the progress you have already made on that design.

Templates

Clicking on Templates will allow you to set a template to help you visualize and work with sizing. It is very handy for someone who is not familiar with Cricut joy Design Space and doesn't know what sizes to set. If you are cutting out wearable items on fabric, you can change the template's size to fit whoever will be wearing it. I'm sure you can agree that this feature is especially beneficial for the seamstresses out there.

Projects

Meanwhile, projects will lead you to the ready-to-make projects so that you can start cutting right away. Some of the projects are not customizable, but others are when you open the template, which is pretty cool. Many of these are not free either, which irks me to a new extent. You can choose the "Free for Cricut (whatever machine you have)", and the projects that will turn up won't have to be paid for.

Text

The Text goes without saying. When you select this option, you can type whatever you want and scale it onto your canvas. You may select any font saved in your computer too; that's why collecting those has never been more useful! There is also an option called "multi-layered font", which gives your text a shadow layer. If you are cutting out the letters and shadow layers, the Cricut will do them separately and combine the two later if you wish to. It can create very cool effects so make sure you try that option out. Furthermore, remember that when you are being paid to do a job, the font you are using might require a license to use.

Shapes

Shapes lets you add basic forms to your canvas, which you can tweak to fit your own needs. The shapes include circle, square, rectangle, triangle, et cetera.

Cricut Basic

This is a program or software designed to help the new user get an easy start designing new crafts and DIY projects. This system will help you with image selection to cutting with the least amount of time spent in the design stages. You can locate your image, pre-set projector font, and immediately print, cut, score, and align with tools found within the program. You can use this program on the iOS 7.1.2 or later systems and iPad and several of the iPhones from the Mini to the 5th generation iPod touch. Since it is also a cloud-based service, you can start in one device and finish from another.

Cricut Sync

You just connect your system to the computer and run the synced program to install updates on the features that come with your machine. This is also used to troubleshoot many issues that could arise from the hardware.

Play Around and Practice

You can combine your shapes and images, add some text, and create patterns. The possibilities are endless. The best thing to do is familiarize yourself with the software before you attempt on cutting expensive materials. Start small and cheap - printer paper will be an ideal choice - and cut away. See what works well for you and stick with it. There are many options concerning the Cricut Design Space. The only way to learn all of this is to experiment and click on every tab you see and try different combinations of options when playing around on the software.

Making Your First Project Idea

According to the instruction, there will be directions on your screen that you must follow to create your first project after setting up your Cricut joy machine. You will still be using the link you found on the paper when you were setting up your machine. If you have not yet received your machine and are interested in knowing how it works, or you are looking for extra clarifications, here's what it will say.

First Step

First off, load a pen into the accessories clamp. You can pick whichever color you think will go best with the paper you have received. Next, you want to turn the knob so that the indicator is pointed to "cardstock," considering that is what you will be working with. Have you had a proper look at your mats yet? The blue mat is what you will want to use for this project. You should remove the plastic cover - keep it, don't throw it away as you will need to recover your mat when you're done to avoid dust accumulation - and lay down the paper on the mat with the top left corners of the material and the grid aligned.

Second Step

Make sure that the paper is pressed flat before you push it between the rollers firmly. The mat has to rest on the bottom roller. When it is in place, press the "Load" button to load your mat between the rollers. Press the "go" button, which will be flashing at this stage, and wait for the machine to work its magic on your project. Once everything is done, the light will flash, and you can press the "Load" button again to unload the mat. Your paper will still be sticking to the mat when you remove it.

Third Step

Be careful when removing the material from the mat. Don't be too hasty; take your time so that it doesn't tear. Pull the mat away from the cardstock instead of doing it the other way around. After completing that step, you can now fold the cardstock in half, insert the liners into the corner slots of the card, and it's done!

You have just made your first ever Cricut project in a matter of minutes from start to finish! Congratulations! What are you waiting for? Do more projects! There are a ton of templates you can play around with—practice, practice, practice.

Always keep in mind when starting a new project that you must first have all of the materials necessary to complete the project. It is always helpful to check your stock of tools and materials before getting started. The worst feeling is when you sit down and begin working on a problematic project only to realize you are out of a specific material needed to finish the job. It will save you a lot of time in the long run if you spend a few minutes at the beginning taking stock of your inventory! Working with materials you already have on hand is also a great way to keep your crafting costs low. It will always feel good to know that you made a custom piece of work without spending a ton of extra money just to complete it!

How to Upload Images with A Cricut Joy

For this method to operate, you will need to upload a picture from your desktop. Click complicated once you upload it, and the next window is where the magic takes place.

At the left corner of the top. Look at the wand? Click on it and press on the hair. Click on the continuation button and name the picture. Click the save button.

It's gone, and it's been so simple. Now, let's look after her flesh. First press back on the magic wand to remove the face, arms, body, and any hard-to-reach pieces. Once you've finished that, take the eraser to wash the remainder of your flesh until it's gone.

Click Continue, identify your picture, and then press Save when the image is to your liking.

Insert both pictures into the surface of your Cricut Design Space. You can bring them back together once you've got them there. One reason I'm excited about this process is that sometimes, like the hair color, I want to change things. I couldn't change the hair color if I left the picture like it was. But I can do that now.

Would you like to know how to edit images in Cricut Design Space as thrilled as I am? I pray so.

Now, go out and do some crafting!

Cut Vinyl with a Cricut Joy

Before cutting, ensure that your Circuit joy machine is set to the right setting to cut vinyl. You can select a thin vinyl setting or set the cut to a thicker level, just to ensure that the Cricut joy machine cuts through the vinyl on the first go-round. You will want to back to stay intact, however (this will make weeding a lot easier when you get to this in the next stop) so don't overdo the cut pressure once you are secure in your vinyl placement on the mat, as well as your machine setting, you are ready to go! Once the mat is loaded and the cut button on your Cricut joy Machine is blinking, you are ready to hit the button and begin cutting. Design Space will give you a percentage as to how far into the project it has cut.

How to Make Stickers

How to Make Safari Animal Sticker

Supplies needed are as follows:

- Cricut machine
- Printable sticker paper

- Inkjet prints

Follow the next few steps to create this sticker:

- Load your Cricut design space page and start a new project.
- Click on Upload Images and upload the images of the animal you want. This is an image gotten online.
- Highlight the whole image and use the Flatten button to solidify the image as a whole.
- Resize the image to the appropriate size you desire. You do the residence by clicking on the image, then drag the right side of the box to the size you desire.
- Click Save at the top left to save your project. Save it to be a print and cut image, after which you click the Make It button at the right hand of the screen.
- Examine the end result and make necessary adjustment where you deem it fit. Click Continue after the adjustment. This will lead you to print the design onto the sticker paper.
- Adjust the dial settings on the Cricut machine to the required settings.
- Set the sticker paper on the cutting mat.

- Load the cutting mat into the machine, and push it against the rollers.

- Press the Load/Unload button and then the Go button to cut the stickers.

How to Make Vinyl Sticker Car Window

Supplies needed are as follows:

- Cricut machine

- Premium outdoor glossy vinyl

- Transfer tape

- Scraper tool

Follow these steps to create:

- Get and save the image you want to use online.

- Log in to the Cricut design space and start a new project.

- Click on the Upload icon and upload the saved image.

- Click on the image and drag to the next page, then select image type.

- Select the parts of the image you do not want as part of the final cut.

- Select the image as a cute image. You will get to preview the image as a cut image.

- Approve the cut image. You would be redirected to the first upload screen.

- Click on your just finished cut file, then highlight it and insert the image.

- The image is added to your design space for size readjusting. The image is ready to cut.

- Cut the image, and remove excessive vinyl after the image is cut.

- Apply a layer of transfer tape to the top of the cut vinyl.

- Clean the car window really well with rubbing alcohol to remove all dirt.

- Carefully peel away the paperback of the vinyl.

- Apply the cut vinyl on the window. Start at one end and roll it down.

- Go over the applied vinyl with a scraper tool to remove air bubble underneath the vinyl.

- Slowly peel away the transfer tape from the window.

<u>Steps for Making Ice-Cream Stickers</u>

The supplies needed for this are as follows:

- Cricut machine

- Printable sticker paper

- Inkjet printer

Steps to making an ice-cream sticker:

- Log in to the Cricut design spaces.

- Start a new project and click on the Images at the screen's left side. Select the ice-cream image(s) you want.

- Highlight the whole image and use the Flatten button to solidify the image as one whole piece.

- Resize the image to the appropriate size you need. You realize this by clicking on the image then dragging the right side of the box to the size you desire.

- Click Save at the top left to save your project. Save it to be a print and cut image, after which you click the Make It button at the right hand of the screen.

- Examine the result and click Continue if it's what you expected. This will lead you to print the design onto the paper.

- Adjust the dial on the Cricut machine to the required settings.
- Place the sticker paper on the cutting mat.
- Load the cutting mat into the machine, and push it against the rollers.
- Press the Load/Unload button and then the Go button to cut the stickers.
- Sit back and let the machine print out your designed sticker.

Working With Images/Edit Panel

Have you tried to find out how to edit pictures in the layout room of Cricut? Also me. Usually

Editing Images In Cricut joy Using The Slice Tool

To assist me in editing pictures in the Cricut Design Space, I used the Slice device. I'm likely still going to use that method for photos I've already uploaded to Cricut Design Space. Let me explain how to edit images using the Slice tool.

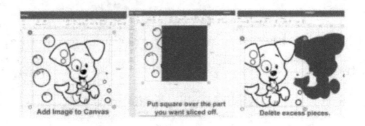

Click on the picture and then click Insert Images to add your attached picture to your Cricut joy canvas. You can add more than one image to your canvas at a time.

Make your picture a lot larger so you can work on it by pressing and pulling it down a little bit on the right upper corner. Just far enough to be able to see it better.

Unlock the table by pressing below the square on the left upper panel. Do you see the icon of the lock? Click on that. Now, using the right top corner, you can transfer the square in any form you want. I placed the circle over the portion that I was about to wipe out, the dog.

Clicking or highlighting the circle, click and hold the change key on your keyboard. Click the picture of the bubble with your mouse, well, bubble for me. This emphasizes both of them.

Click the Slice device at the right upper corner with both the circle and the picture outlined.

Start taking back your slice's parts. There ought to be three parts. They can be deleted.

Continue this method until the manner you want your picture to be printed.

Cricut Scrapbooking

Scrapbooking is a technique of preserving memories that has existed for quite a while and has developed a lot. In past times, the development of one scrapbook was a monumentally outrageous job.

However, with the creation of products like the Cricut cutting machine, things are a lot easier. If you are looking into developing a scrapbook, this poor boy will be the tool for you. You will find lots of great Cricut suggestions in this book that you can make the most of.

Scrapbooks are simply several of the numerous Cricut suggestions. This tool, in case you know the way to maximize it can enable you to make things go beyond scrapbooking like calendars.

If you purchase a Cricut cartridge, you will find a load of designs uploaded in each one. These pre-created themes are usually utilized for a wide range of items like hangings for walls, picture frames, and greeting cards for those seasons.

Just your imagination is going to limit your progress with a Cricut piece of equipment. With calendars, you can design every month to reflect special events, the mood, and the weather which are associated with it.

The Cricut device can handle that. But in the event that an individual cartridge doesn't keep design which needs, you can constantly go and purchase. It is that simple!

Cricut devices could be a bit costly with the price beginning at 1dolar1 299. That is hefty for anyone to begin with. Be a sensible customer. You can often turn to the web to search for deals that are great on Cricut machines.

Everything now appears to be extremely convenient. Should you look for labor now, the majority has become machine intensive instead of labor-intensive. It doesn't mean suggesting that today, leave the machines and allow them to perform the work.

They nevertheless need the working prowess of individuals. I never wish it involves that time where devices are self - operating.

The art of scrapbook making is but one facet of human civilization, which has become a lot easier due to engineering merchandise, especially the Cricut cutting machine. It is at this time which Cricut scrapbooking takes the center stage.

In case you are considering of putting in the Cricut scrapbooking world, this device is a must-have. You cannot say no and just claim that I can do it by hand because doing this will drive you to the cliff and into the jaws of insanity.

Utilizing Shape Cartridge helps you develop shapes like animals, tags, boxes, dolls, and hearts amongst others. Pick these cutout symbols to embellish your scrapbook for a fascinating remembrance on your own or a present for someone very special.

Solving the most common problem when using Cricut Joy

Does the Cricut Maker cut fabric patterns such as clothes, pants, shirts, skirts, blouses etc.?

Absolutely Yes, the Cricut Machine can cut through fabric patterns the Cricut Maker comes with 25 patters for sewing to assist you to get started. In addition the Cricut Maker comes with hundreds of design patterns in collaboration with Simplicity.

Does the Cricut Maker etch through glass?

Yes, the Cricut maker can etch glass but not directly. To do this you need to create and cut your own design patterns using the Design space and applying an etching cream onto the glass surface.

Do I lose my projects, uploaded images and cartridges when upgrading the Cricut Maker?

No. Your projects, cartridges and uploaded images remain intact the reason being because you typically use a Cricut ID in the Cricut cloud and not machines with the same Cricut ID and not the machine itself. So you can be sure all you content will be accessible with the Cricut Maker.

Does the Cricut Maker engrave metallic materials such as jewellery or Pet ID tags?

Yes, but to technically achieve this you need a special etching tool for it to go through a third party. This is because the deep engraving functionality may fail on some metallic objects. Among such tools you may need is an etching tool by "Chomas creation" which fits into the Cricut Maker as other tools. With the tool, you can engrave or etch material such as leather, metal clay, silver, aluminum, bronze, copper, plastic, and acrylic

Do I need a printer? What printer should I use?

Absolutely No, Cricut joy machines are not dependent upon printers.

As far as what printer to get, you just need something that prints color! Some of the most versatile Hp machine is the HP Envy, but there are many great printers out there in the market that are not limited to Hp.

Does there exist any difference in the power Cords of the Cricut joy Machine?

No, there is a physical difference in the Power cords of the Cricut joy Machines. However, there is a difference in the output current with the Cricut joy cord upgraded to supply 3A with its predecessors—Cricut Explore having a 2.5A output current supply. This adaption also allows you to charge your mobile phone via its charging port on the right-hand side while multitasking the cutting/writing functionalities.

However if you using the Cricut Explore you can still charge the mobile phone device. Still, the difference is that because of its low current capacity it will either slow, stutter or even shut off (in extreme cases) because the device will need a current supply and the cutting operation —which needs more current supply especially as it requires more cutting pressure.

What materials can I cut using the Cricut joy?

The Cricut engineering team is in the process of experimenting more materials, cutting pressures and guidelines. However the following are some of the materials it cuts; fabric, papers—crepe and tissue, vinyl, cardstock, cork, leather, duct tape, faux leather, chipboard, felt, adhesive foil, among others.

How does the Rotary cutter differ with the fabric blade?

The Cricut Maker can use both, the rotary blade, and the bonded fabric blade. However the difference is that the rotary blade can cut through delicate materials without a backing material. In contrast, the rotary blade will need to use the Adaptive tool system to perform the precision cutting experience.

What is the Pink Mat and how can I use it?

The Pink Mat is useful for cutting fabrics as well as other delicate materials. It is highly durable therefore strong which means it can withstand pressure when cutting thin materials. You may be asking how it needs a strong material whereas the material under cut is thin. It takes a lot of pressure when cutting delicate materials meaning it needs to stay flat on the mat to resist the need to shift.

Are blades and tools of the Cricut joy and other predecessors interchangeable?

Yes and No. The tools of the Cricut joy cannot be used in the Cricut Explore machines however the blades of the Cricut Maker can be used by the Cricut Explore machines. Simply the reason being the Cricut joy came after the Cricut Explore therefore the functionalities of the Cricut Explore differ with that the Cricut joy with the latter being more advanced compared to the Explore. It does not have the drive gears that control the rotary blade and knife, for starters, and the pressure required to operate these tools are simply not present in the Explore.

How does the Cricut joy differ with its predecessors in terms of the software?

Both are similar in terms of software because they use the Cricut Design space. This means that all the Explore projects can be cut by the Cricut joy whereas some project by Cricut Maker can be also be cut by the Cricut Explore as long as it does not concern the rotary and knife blades.

Chapter 4: FAQs about the Cricut Maker & Joy

Why does Design Space say my Cricut machine is already in use when it's not?

To resolve this, make sure that you've completed the New Machine Setup for your Cricut. Try Design Space in another browser. The two that work best are Google Chrome and Mozilla Firefox; if it doesn't work in one of those, try the other. If that doesn't clear the error, try a different USB port and USB cable. Disconnect the machine from the computer and turn it off. While it's off, restart your computer. After your computer restarts, reconnect the machine and turn it on. Wait a few moments, and then try Design Space again. If you're still having the same problem, contact Cricut Member Care.

Why doesn't my cut match the preview in Design Space?

Test another image and see if the same thing happens. If it's only happening with the one project, create a new project and start over or try a different image. If it happens with a second project, and your machine is connected with Bluetooth, disconnect that and plug it in with a USB cable. Larger projects may sometimes have difficulty communicating the cuts over Bluetooth. If you can't connect with USB or the problem is still occurring, check that your computer matches or exceeds the running Design Space system requirements. If it doesn't, try the project on a different computer or mobile device that does. If your computer does meet the requirements, open Design Space in a different browser and try again. If the problem continues, try a different USB cable. Finally, if the issue still hasn't resolved, contact Cricut Member Care.

What do I do if I need to install USB drivers for my Cricut machine?

Typically, the Cricut drivers are automatically installed when you connect it with a USB cable. If Design Space doesn't see your machine, you can try this to troubleshoot the driver installation. First, open Device Manager on your computer. You'll need to have administrator rights. For Windows 7, click Start, right-click on Computer, and select Manage.

Why does my Cricut Maker say the blade is not detected?

Make sure that the tool in Clamp B is the same one Design Space recommends in the Load Tools step of the Project Preview screen. If you don't have that recommended tool, unload your mat and select Edit Tools on the Project Preview screen. Here, you can select a different tool. If the tool and the selection already match, carefully remove the tool from Clamp B and clean the reflective band on the housing. Reinstall it in the clamp and press the Go button. If that doesn't resolve the problem, remove the tool again and clean the machine's sensor. Reinstall the tool and press Go again.

Why is my Cricut machine making a grinding noise?

If it's the carriage car making a loud noise after you press the cut button, and it sounds like the carriage might be hitting the side of the machine, record a short video of it and send it to Cricut Member Care. If the noise comes from a brand-new machine the first time you use it, contact Cricut Member Care. Otherwise, make sure that you're using the original power cord that came with your machine. If the machine isn't getting the correct voltage, it may produce a grinding sound. If you are using the machine's power cord, adjust your pressure settings. If it's too high, it might produce an unusual sound. Decrease it in increments of 2–4, and do some test cuts. If it's still making the issue even after decreasing the cutting pressure, contact Cricut Member Care.

Why is my mat going into the machine crooked?

Check the roller bar to see if it's loose, damaged, or uneven. If it is, take a photo or video of it to send to Cricut Member Care. If the roller bar seems fine, make sure that you're using the right mat size for the machine. Make sure the mat is correctly lined up with the guides and that the edge is underneath the roller bar when you prepare to load it. If it's still loading crookedly even when properly lined up with the guides, try applying gentle pressure to the mat to get it under the roller bar once it starts. If none of this works, contact Cricut Member Care.

Why isn't the Smart Set Dial changing the material in Design Space?

Make sure that the USB cable between the computer and the Cricut Explore is properly connected. If so, disconnect the Explorer from the computer and turn it off. Restart your computer. Once it's on, turn on the Explore, plug it into the computer, and try the cut again. If it still isn't changing the material, connect the USB cable to a different port on the computer. If it's still not working, try Design Space in multiple web browsers and see if the problem replicates. If it does, try an entirely different USB cable. Check for Firmware Updates for the Explore. If you don't have another USB cable, the Firmware Update doesn't help, or there are no Firmware Updates, contact Cricut Member Care.

What do I do if my Cricut Maker stopped partway through a cut?

If the Knife Blade stops cutting and the Go button are flashing, the Maker has encountered some error. In Design Space, you'll get a notification that the blade is stuck. This might have been caused by the blade running into something like a knot or seam if too much dust or debris built up in the cut area or if the blade got into a gouge in the mat from a previous cut. To resume your project, do not unload the mat. This will lose your place in the project, and it will be impossible to get it lined up again. Check the cut area for dust or debris, and gently clean it.

Why is my fabric getting caught under the rollers?

Be sure to cut down any fabric so that it fits on your mat without going past the adhesive. If you have stuck the fabric and realize it's hanging past the adhesive, use a ruler and a sharp blade to trim it. Or, if it's the correct size but slightly askew, unstick it and reposition it.

Why would my Cricut Maker continuously turn off during cuts?

This can happen from a build-up of static electricity while cutting foil and metal sheets. Makers in dry areas are more susceptible to this. Spritzing water in the air will dissipate the build-up. Be careful not to spray any water directly on the Maker. Using a humidifier or vaporizer in the area where you use your Maker can help avoid the static build-ups. If this doesn't seem to be what's causing the issue, contact Cricut Member Care.

Chapter 5: Tips that might Assist You To Begin

If you can you can subscribe to the access for about ten dollars a month to gain access to over twenty thousand different images and over a thousand different projects. You even get over three hundred fonts.

You will also need to keep the plastic sheets that come with the mats to protect them between your uses.

Clean your cutting mats with baby wipes that are water-based to keep them sticky and clean longer.

Use one blade for your cardstock and a separate one for vinyl because this will let them both last longer.

Make sure that you have a deep cut blade.

This is for people who have had the cartridges for an older machine or older cartridge. You can hook these up to your new account. It is a simple thing to do but you should know that you could only link

117

them once so be sure that if you are buying a machine second hand, nothing has been linked yet.

The right tools are important here so you should make sure that you have the toolset. It will contain vital tools that you need, and they can especially help with vinyl.

Know your glue

Many people are huge fans of what is called tacky glue. It gives your projects a little bit of wiggle room when you're trying to position them. The problem is that it can take longer to dry. If this is something that bothers you, you might want to try a quicker one. Zip dry paper glue it's extremely sticky and much faster.

A tip that will go along with the tip above is that you want them to be a layer to pop out from another layer. You can make this happen by using products like pop dots or Zots. They are self-adhesive foam mounts. You can also make little circles using craft foam or cardboard and then glue it between the layers.

Think about a Coach

Business mentors are extremely popular nowadays. Consider going through some cash with a Scrapbooking business mentor who comprehends the business as well as genuinely comprehends the specific brand of energy scrapbook sweethearts share. A mentor can help share business abilities however can go about as an extraordinary coach in managing you to your objectives.

Exhibit Your True Talent with a Business Card for Artists

The financial downturn has left huge numbers of us feeling the squeeze. Numerous individuals are searching for approaches to set aside cash in each part of life. Be that as it may, there are times when a buy must be made, and cautious research regularly structures some portion of the basic leadership the procedure.

Give the Quality of Your Work a chance to radiate through

A business card for specialists is your window to the world, and it should say a great deal regarding your aesthetic edge and abilities. Make it state every little thing about you and what you can offer. Plan a motivating logo that can join the substance of what you can do with an incredible structure. This astute connecting can put you on top of things by helping individuals to recollect who and what you are.

Consider Other Ways You Can Display Your Skills to the World

A business card for specialists is only one of numerous limited time apparatuses you can use to enhance your presentation. It bodes well. The production of a notice is a magnificent method to demonstrate the best of what you do. Try not to place a lot into your sign; that will go about as an obstacle and prevent individuals from getting a vibe of your actual abilities. Consider the area where you can show your blurb. Vital arranging of the setting of your sign can help augment its effect. It will expand the intrigue of your work and open up more potential outcomes.

Remember to tell individuals how to connect!

A business card for specialists needs not exclusively to demonstrate the embodiment of your innovativeness; it likewise fills a need. It needs to tell potential clients how to connect with you. Incorporate all the distinctive contact techniques you have, email, site, telephone numbers, and any online networking you are an individual from. Remember the intensity of internet based life and bookmarking destinations; they can enable feature to considerably a greater amount of your work.

Be Adaptable

Consider chipping away at zones that you hadn't imagined, however will be something inside your abilities. This will enable you to set up notoriety. Another viable method to advance your aptitudes notwithstanding utilizing a business card for specialists is to engage in network ventures where you offer your administrations for nothing. Make something stunning that individuals will see every day; this is an incredible advert for your aptitudes. This will place your work into thousands of individuals' lives and drive more clients to you.

Conclusion

In this book, we have given you the tools to make your Cricut work at its best all day every day. When you can do this, you will be able to make anything that you want because these machines can cut amazingly well and they have so many functions that it could make your head spin. This book has been able to help you see the difference between the different machines and how and why the prices are different. Each machine has something that it does best and the Maker is the best of the four as it can cut more than any other machine. This means that you get to work with new materials that you will not use with the other machines because they can't cut it. They call the Maker the ultimate machine because it can do what others can't.

When you choose the machine that will work best with you, you will find that the website from the company itself is much cheaper than the other retailers that you can find online. The benefit from buying from the company itself is that you do not have to deal with a third party. Instead, you get coupons, bundles and discounts that you are looking for, and there is no problem with the machine. In addition to that, when you buy from a third party retailer, they do not let you bundle at all so you will be paying an extra per item you want. This can get very expensive very quickly.

We also give you great advice on projects that you can do with your particular machine. There are somethings that individual devices can cut and others can't cut very much. If you are doing heavy-duty projects, you will need a machine that can do this. This is why we have compiled the best information for you.

Thank you for downloading this book